LAO TZU

TAO TE CHING

LAO TZU

TAO TE CHING

A Book about the Way and the Power of the Way

An English Version by
Ursula K. Le Guin

WITH THE COLLABORATION OF
J. P. Seaton, Professor of Chinese,
University of North Carolina, Chapel Hill

SHAMBHALA
Boulder
2019

SHAMBHALA PUBLICATIONS, INC.
2129 13th Street
Boulder, Colorado 80302
www.shambhala.com

14   13   12   11   10   9   8   7

Printed in the United States of America

Shambhala Publications makes every effort to print on acid-free,
recycled paper.

Shambhala Publications is distributed worldwide by
Penguin Random House, Inc., and its subsidiaries.

The Library of Congress catalogues the original edition of this book as follows:
Lao-tzu.
[Tao te ching.   English]
Lao Tzu: Tao te ching: a book about the way and the power of the way/
a new English version by Ursula K. Le Guin, with J. P. Seaton.
—1st ed.
p.   cm.
ISBN 978-1-57062-333-2 (hardcover)
ISBN 978-1-61180-724-0
I. Le Guin, Ursula K., 1929–   . II. Seaton, Jerome P.
III. Title.
BL 1900.L26E5   1997a   97-18942
299'.51482—dc21

FOR A. L. K. AND J. P. S.

CONTENTS

INTRODUCTION

The *Tao Te Ching* was probably written about twenty-five hundred years ago, perhaps by a man called Lao Tzu, who may have lived at about the same time as Confucius. Nothing about it is certain except that it's Chinese, and very old, and speaks to people everywhere as if it had been written yesterday.

The first *Tao Te Ching* I ever saw was the Paul Carus edition of 1898, bound in yellow cloth stamped with blue and red Chinese designs and characters. It was a venerable object of mystery, which I soon investigated, and found more fascinating inside than out. The book was my father's; he read in it often. Once I saw him making notes from it and asked what he was doing. He said he was marking which chapters he'd like to have read at his funeral. We did read those chapters at his memorial service.

I have the book, now ninety-eight years old and further ornamented with red binding-tape to hold the back on, and have marked which chapters I'd like to have read at my funeral. In the Notes, I explain why I was so lucky to discover Lao Tzu in that particular edition. Here I will only say that I was lucky to discover him so young, so that I could live with his book my whole life long.

I also discuss other aspects of my version in the Notes—the how of it. Here I want to state very briefly the why of it.

The *Tao Te Ching* is partly in prose, partly in verse; but as we define poetry now, not by rhyme and meter but as a patterned intensity of language, the whole thing is poetry. I wanted to catch that poetry, its terse, strange beauty. Most translations have caught meanings in their net, but prosily, letting the beauty slip through. And in poetry, beauty is no ornament; it is the meaning. It is the truth. We have that on good authority.

Scholarly translations of the *Tao Te Ching* as a manual for rulers use a vocabulary that emphasizes the uniqueness of the Taoist "sage," his masculinity, his authority. This language is perpetuated, and degraded, in most popular versions. I wanted a Book of the Way accessible to a present-day, unwise, unpowerful, and perhaps unmale reader, not seeking esoteric secrets, but listening for a voice that speaks to the soul. I would like that reader to see why people have loved the book for twenty-five hundred years.

It is the most lovable of all the great religious texts, funny, keen, kind, modest, indestructibly outrageous, and inexhaustibly refreshing. Of all the deep springs, this is the purest water. To me, it is also the deepest spring.

—*Ursula K. Le Guin*

Commentaries at the foot of some of the chapters are my own responses to the text. They are idiosyncratic and unscholarly, and are to be ignored if not found helpful. In the Notes at the end of the book are more detailed considerations of some of the chapters, thanks to my sources and guides, and remarks on how I arrived at my version.

Book One

TAOING

The way you can go
isn't the real way.
The name you can say
isn't the real name.

Heaven and earth
begin in the unnamed:
name's the mother
of the ten thousand things.

So the unwanting soul
sees what's hidden,
and the ever-wanting soul
sees only what it wants.

Two things, one origin,
but different in name,
whose identity is mystery.
Mystery of all mysteries!
The door to the hidden.

A satisfactory translation of this chapter is, I believe, perfectly impossible. It contains the book. I think of it as the Aleph, in Borges's story: if you see it rightly, it contains everything.

SOUL FOOD

Everybody on earth knowing
that beauty is beautiful
makes ugliness.

Everybody knowing
that goodness is good
makes wickedness.

For being and nonbeing
arise together;
hard and easy
complete each other;
long and short
shape each other;
high and low
depend on each other;
note and voice
make the music together;
before and after
follow each other.

That's why the wise soul
does without doing,
teaches without talking.

The things of this world
exist, they are;
you can't refuse them.

To bear and not to own;
to act and not lay claim;
to do the work and let it go:
for just letting it go
is what makes it stay.

One of the things I read in this chapter is that values and beliefs are
not only culturally constructed but also part of the interplay of yin and
yang, the great reversals that maintain the living balance of the world.
To believe that our beliefs are permanent truths which encompass reality is a sad arrogance. To let go of that belief is to find safety.

HUSHING

Not praising the praiseworthy
keeps people uncompetitive.

Not prizing rare treasures
keeps people from stealing.

Not looking at the desirable
keeps the mind quiet.

So the wise soul
governing people
would empty their minds,
fill their bellies,
weaken their wishes,
strengthen their bones,
keep people unknowing,
unwanting,
keep the ones who do know
from doing anything.

When you do not-doing,
nothing's out of order.

Over and over Lao Tzu says *wei wu wei*: Do not do. Doing not-doing. To act without acting. Action by inaction. You do nothing yet it gets done. . . .

It's not a statement susceptible to logical interpretation, or even to a syntactical translation into English; but it's a concept that transforms thought radically, that changes minds. The whole book is both an explanation and a demonstration of it.

SOURCELESS

The way is empty,
used, but not used up.
Deep, yes! ancestral
to the ten thousand things.

Blunting edge,
loosing bond,
dimming light,
the way is the dust of the way.

Quiet,
yes, and likely to endure.
Whose child? born
before the gods.

4

Everything Lao Tzu says is elusive. The temptation is to grasp at something tangible in the endlessly deceptive simplicity of the words. Even some of his finest scholarly translators focus on positive ethical or political values in the text, as if those were what's important in it. And of course the religion called Taoism is full of gods, saints, miracles, prayers, rules, methods for securing riches, power, longevity, and so forth—all the stuff that Lao Tzu says leads us away from the Way.

In passages such as this one, I think it is the profound modesty of the language that offers what so many people for so many centuries have found in this book: a pure apprehension of the mystery of which we are part.

USEFUL EMPTINESS

5

Heaven and earth aren't humane.
To them the ten thousand things
are straw dogs.

Wise souls aren't humane.
To them the hundred families
are straw dogs.

Heaven and earth
act as a bellows:

Empty yet structured,
it moves, inexhaustibly giving.

The "inhumanity" of the wise soul doesn't mean cruelty. Cruelty is
a human characteristic. Heaven and earth—that is, "Nature" and its
Way—are not humane, because they are not human. They are not
kind; they are not cruel: those are human attributes. You can only be
kind or cruel if you have, and cherish, a self. You can't even be indiffer-
ent if you aren't different. Altruism is the other side of egoism. Followers of the Way, like the forces of nature, act selflessly.

WHAT IS COMPLETE

The valley spirit never dies.
Call it the mystery, the woman.

The mystery,
the Door of the Woman,
is the root
of earth and heaven.

Forever this endures, forever.
And all its uses are easy.

6

DIM BRIGHTNESS

7

Heaven will last,
earth will endure.
How can they last so long?
They don't exist for themselves
and so can go on and on.

So wise souls
leaving self behind
move forward,
and setting self aside
stay centered.
Why let the self go?
To keep what the soul needs.

EASY BY NATURE

True goodness
is like water.
Water's good
for everything.
It doesn't compete.

It goes right
to the low loathsome places,
and so finds the way.

For a house,
the good thing is level ground.
In thinking,
depth is good.
The good of giving is magnanimity;
of speaking, honesty;
of government, order.
The good of work is skill,
and of action, timing.

No competition,
so no blame.

A clear stream of water runs through this book, from poem to poem,
wearing down the indestructible, finding the way around everything
that obstructs the way. Good drinking water.

BEING QUIET

9

Brim-fill the bowl,
it'll spill over.
Keep sharpening the blade,
you'll soon blunt it.

Nobody can protect
a house full of gold and jade.

Wealth, status, pride,
are their own ruin.
To do good, work well, and lie low
is the way of the blessing.

TECHNIQUES

Can you keep your soul in its body,
hold fast to the one,
and so learn to be whole?
Can you center your energy,
be soft, tender,
and so learn to be a baby?

Can you keep the deep water still and clear,
so it reflects without blurring?
Can you love people and run things,
and do so by not doing?

Opening, closing the Gate of Heaven,
can you be like a bird with her nestlings?
Piercing bright through the cosmos,
can you know by not knowing?

To give birth, to nourish,
to bear and not to own,
to act and not lay claim,
to lead and not to rule:
this is mysterious power.

Most of the scholars think this chapter is about meditation, its techniques and fulfillments. The language is profoundly mystical, the images are charged, rich in implications.

The last verse turns up in nearly the same words in other chapters; there are several such "refrains" throughout the book, identical or similar lines repeated once or twice or three times.

THE USES OF NOT

Thirty spokes
meet in the hub.
Where the wheel isn't
is where it's useful.

Hollowed out,
clay makes a pot.
Where the pot's not
is where it's useful.

Cut doors and windows
to make a room.
Where the room isn't,
there's room for you.

So the profit in what is
is in the use of what isn't.

One of the things I love about Lao Tzu is he is so funny. He's explaining a profound and difficult truth here, one of those counterintuitive truths that, when the mind can accept them, suddenly double the size of the universe. He goes about it with this deadpan simplicity, talking about pots.

NOT WANTING

The five colors
blind our eyes.
The five notes
deafen our ears.
The five flavors
dull our taste.

Racing, chasing, hunting,
drives people crazy.
Trying to get rich
ties people in knots.

So the wise soul
watches with the inner
not the outward eye,
letting that go,
keeping this.

SHAMELESS

To be in favor or disgrace
is to live in fear.
To take the body seriously
is to admit one can suffer.

What does that mean,
to be in favor or disgrace
is to live in fear?
Favor debases:
we fear to lose it,
fear to win it.
So to be in favor or disgrace
is to live in fear.

What does that mean,
to take the body seriously
is to admit one can suffer?
I suffer because I'm a body;
if I weren't a body,
how could I suffer?

So people who set their bodily good
before the public good
could be entrusted with the commonwealth,
and people who treated the body politic
as gently as their own body
would be worthy to govern the commonwealth.

Lao Tzu, a mystic, demystifies political power.

Autocracy and oligarchy foster the beliefs that power is gained magically and retained by sacrifice, and that powerful people are genuinely superior to the powerless.

Lao Tzu does not see political power as magic. He sees rightful power as earned and wrongful power as usurped. He does not see power as virtue, but as the result of virtue. The democracies are founded on that view.

He sees sacrifice of self or others as a corruption of power, and power as available to anybody who follows the Way. This is a radically subversive attitude. No wonder anarchists and Taoists make good friends.

CELEBRATING MYSTERY

14

Look at it: nothing to see.
Call it colorless.
Listen to it: nothing to hear.
Call it soundless.
Reach for it: nothing to hold.
Call it intangible.

Triply undifferentiated,
it merges into oneness,
not bright above,
not dark below.

Never, oh! never
can it be named.
It reverts, it returns
to unbeing.
Call it the form of the unformed,
the image of no image.

Call it unthinkable thought.
Face it: no face.
Follow it: no end.

Holding fast to the old Way,
we can live in the present.
Mindful of the ancient beginnings,
we hold the thread of the Tao.

PEOPLE OF POWER

Once upon a time

people who knew the Way
were subtle, spiritual, mysterious, penetrating,
unfathomable.

Since they're inexplicable
I can only say what they seemed like:
Cautious, oh yes, as if wading through a winter
     river.
Alert, as if afraid of the neighbors.
Polite and quiet, like houseguests.
Elusive, like melting ice.
Blank, like uncut wood.
Empty, like valleys.
Mysterious, oh yes, they were like troubled water.

Who can by stillness, little by little
make what is troubled grow clear?
Who can by movement, little by little
make what is still grow quick?
To follow the Way
is not to need fulfillment.
Unfulfilled, one may live on
needing no renewal.

In the first stanza we see the followers of the Way in ancient times or
illo tempore, remote and inaccessible; but the second stanza brings
them close and alive in a series of marvelous similes. (I am particularly
fond of the polite and quiet houseguests.) The images of the valley and
of uncut or uncarved wood will recur again and again.

RETURNING TO THE ROOT

16

Be completely empty.
Be perfectly serene.
The ten thousand things arise together;
in their arising is their return.
Now they flower,
and flowering
sink homeward,
returning to the root.

The return to the root
is peace.
Peace: to accept what must be,
to know what endures.
In that knowledge is wisdom.
Without it, ruin, disorder.

To know what endures
is to be openhearted,
magnanimous,
regal,
blessed,
following the Tao,
the way that endures forever.
The body comes to its ending,
but there is nothing to fear.

To those who will not admit morality without a deity to validate it, or
spirituality of which man is not the measure, the firmness of Lao Tzu's
morality and the sweetness of his spiritual counsel must seem incom-
prehensible, or illegitimate, or very troubling indeed.

ACTING SIMPLY

True leaders
are hardly known to their followers.
Next after them are the leaders
the people know and admire;
after them, those they fear;
after them, those they despise.

To give no trust
is to get no trust.

When the work's done right,
with no fuss or boasting,
ordinary people say,
Oh, we did it.

This invisible leader, who gets things done in such a way that people
think they did it all themselves, isn't one who manipulates others from
behind the scenes; just the opposite. Again, it's a matter of "doing
without doing": uncompetitive, unworried, trustful accomplishment,
power that is not force. An example or analogy might be a very good
teacher, or the truest voice in a group of singers.

SECOND BESTS

18

In the degradation of the great way
come benevolence and righteousness.
With the exaltation of learning and prudence
comes immense hypocrisy.
The disordered family
is full of dutiful children and parents.
The disordered society
is full of loyal patriots.

RAW SILK AND UNCUT WOOD

Stop being holy, forget being prudent,
it'll be a hundred times better for everyone.
Stop being altruistic, forget being righteous,
people will remember what family feeling is.
Stop planning, forget making a profit,
there won't be any thieves and robbers.

But even these three rules
needn't be followed; what works reliably
is to know the raw silk,
hold the uncut wood.
Need little,
want less.
Forget the rules.
Be untroubled.

This chapter and the two before it may be read as a single movement of
thought.

"Raw silk" and "uncut wood" are images traditionally associated
with the characters *su* (simple, plain) and *p'u* (natural, honest).

BEING DIFFERENT

20

How much difference between yes and no?
What difference between good and bad?

What the people fear
must be feared.
O desolation!
Not yet, not yet has it reached its limit!

Everybody's cheerful,
cheerful as if at a party,
or climbing a tower in springtime.
And here I sit unmoved,
clueless, like a child,
a baby too young to smile.

Forlorn, forlorn.
Like a homeless person.
Most people have plenty.
I'm the one that's poor,
a fool right through.

Ignorant, ignorant.
Most people are so bright.
I'm the one that's dull.
Most people are so keen.
I don't have the answers.
Oh, I'm desolate, at sea,
adrift, without harbor.

Everybody has something to do.
I'm the clumsy one, out of place.
I'm the different one,
for my food
is the milk of the mother.

The difference between yes and no, good and bad, is something only the "bright" people, the people with the answers, can understand. A poor stupid Taoist can't make it out.

This chapter is full of words like *huang* (wild, barren; famine), *tun* (ignorant; chaotic), *hun* (dull, turbid), *men* (sad, puzzled, mute), and *hu* (confused, obscured, vague). They configure chaos, confusion, a "bewilderness" in which the mind wanders without certainties, desolate, silent, awkward. But in that milky, dim strangeness lies the way. It can't be found in the superficial order imposed by positive and negative opinions, the good/bad, yes/no moralizing that denies fear and ignores mystery.

THE EMPTY HEART

21

The greatest power is the gift
of following the Way alone.
How the Way does things
is hard to grasp, elusive.
Elusive, yes, hard to grasp,
yet there are thoughts in it.
Hard to grasp, yes, elusive,
yet there are things in it.
Hard to make out, yes, and obscure,
yet there is spirit in it,
veritable spirit.
There is certainty in it.
From long, long ago till now
it has kept its name.
So it saw
the beginning of everything.

How do I know
anything about the beginning?
By this.

Mysticism rises from and returns to the irreducible, unsayable reality of
"this." "This" is the Way. This is the way.

GROWING DOWNWARD

Be broken to be whole.
Twist to be straight.
Be empty to be full.
Wear out to be renewed.
Have little and gain much.
Have much and get confused.

So wise souls hold to the one,
and test all things against it.

Not showing themselves,
they shine forth.
Not justifying themselves,
they're self-evident.
Not praising themselves,
they're accomplished.
Not competing,
they have in all the world no competitor.

What they used to say in the old days,
"Be broken to be whole,"
was that mistaken?
Truly, to be whole
is to return.

NOTHING AND NOT

23

Nature doesn't make long speeches.
A whirlwind doesn't last all morning.
A cloudburst doesn't last all day.
Who makes the wind and rain?
Heaven and earth do.
If heaven and earth don't go on and on,
certainly people don't need to.

The people who work with Tao
are Tao people,
they belong to the Way.
People who work with power
belong to power.
People who work with loss
belong to what's lost.

Give yourself to the Way
and you'll be at home on the Way.
Give yourself to power
and you'll be at home in power.
Give yourself to loss
and when you're lost you'll be at home.

To give no trust
is to get no trust.

PROPORTION

You can't keep standing on tiptoe
or walk in leaps and bounds.
You can't shine by showing off
or get ahead by pushing.
Self-satisfied people do no good,
self-promoters never grow up.

Such stuff is to the Tao
as garbage is to food
or a tumor to the body,
hateful.
The follower of the Way
avoids it.

24

IMAGING MYSTERY

25

There is something
that contains everything.
Before heaven and earth
it is.
Oh, it is still, unbodied,
all on its own, unchanging,

all-pervading,
ever-moving.
So it can act as the mother
of all things.
Not knowing its real name,
we only call it the Way.

If it must be named,
let its name be Great.
Greatness means going on,
going on means going far,
and going far means turning back.

So they say: "The Way is great,
heaven is great,
earth is great,
and humankind is great;
four greatnesses in the world,
and humanity is one of them."

People follow earth,
earth follows heaven,
heaven follows the Way,
the Way follows what is.

I'd like to call the "something" of the first line a lump—an unshaped, undifferentiated lump, chaos, before the Word, before Form, before Change. Inside it is time, space, everything; in the womb of the Way.

The last words of the chapter, *tzu jan*, I render as "what is." I was tempted to say, "The Way follows itself," because the Way is the way things are; but that would reduce the significance of the words. They remind us not to see the Way as a sovereignty or a domination, all creative, all yang. The Way itself is a follower. Though it is before everything, it follows what is.

POWER OF THE HEAVY

26

Heavy is the root of light.
Still is the master of moving.

So wise souls make their daily march
with the heavy baggage wagon.

Only when safe
in a solid, quiet house
do they lay care aside.

How can a lord of ten thousand chariots
let his own person
weigh less in the balance than his land?
Lightness will lose him his foundation,
movement will lose him his mastery.

I take heaviness to be the root matters of daily life, the baggage we
bodily beings have to carry, such as food, drink, shelter, safety. If you go
charging too far ahead of the baggage wagon you may be cut off from it;
if you treat your body as unimportant you risk insanity or inanity.

The first two lines would make a nice motto for the practice of
T'ai Chi.

SKILL

Good walkers leave no track.
Good talkers don't stammer.
Good counters don't use their fingers.
The best door's unlocked and unopened.
The best knot's not in a rope and can't be untied.

So wise souls are good at caring for people,
never turning their back on anyone.
They're good at looking after things,
never turning their back on anything.
There's a light hidden here.

Good people teach people who aren't good yet;
the less good are the makings of the good.
Anyone who doesn't respect a teacher
or cherish a student
may be clever, but has gone astray.
There's a deep mystery here.

The hidden light and the deep mystery seem to be signals, saying
"think about this"—about care for what seems unimportant. In a teacher's parental care for the insignificant student, and in a society's respect
for mothers, teachers, and other obscure people who educate, there
is indeed illumination and a profoundly human mystery. Having re-
placed instinct with language, society, and culture, we are the only spe-
cies that depends on teaching and learning. We aren't human without
them. In them is true power. But are they the occupations of the rich
and mighty?

TURNING BACK

28

Knowing man
and staying woman,
be the riverbed of the world.
Being the world's riverbed
of eternal unfailing power
is to go back again to be newborn.

Knowing light
and staying dark,
be a pattern to the world.
Being the world's pattern
of eternal unerring power
is to go back again to boundlessness.

Knowing glory
and staying modest,
be the valley of the world.
Being the world's valley
of eternal inexhaustible power
is to go back again to the natural.

Natural wood is cut up
and made into useful things.
Wise souls are used
to make into leaders.
Just so, a great carving
is done without cutting.

The simplicity of Lao Tzu's language can present an almost impenetrable density of meaning. The reversals and paradoxes in this great poem are the oppositions of the yin and yang—male/female, light/ dark, glory/modesty—but the "knowing and being" of them, the balancing act, results in neither stasis nor synthesis. The riverbed in which power runs leads back, the patterns of power lead back, the valley where power is contained leads back—to the forever new, endless, straightforward way. Reversal, recurrence, are the movement, and yet the movement is onward.

NOT DOING

Those who think to win the world
by doing something to it,
I see them come to grief.
For the world is a sacred object.
Nothing is to be done to it.
To do anything to it is to damage it.
To seize it is to lose it.

Under heaven some things lead, some follow,
some blow hot, some cold,
some are strong, some weak,
some are fulfilled, some fail.

So the wise soul keeps away
from the extremes, excess, extravagance.

For Lao Tzu, "moderation in all things" isn't just a bit of safe, practical
advice. To lose the sense of the sacredness of the world is a mortal loss.
To injure our world by excesses of greed and ingenuity is to endanger
our own sacredness.

NOT MAKING WAR

A Taoist wouldn't advise a ruler
to use force of arms for conquest;
that tactic backfires.

Where the army marched
grow thorns and thistles.
After the war
come the bad harvests.
Good leaders prosper, that's all,
not presuming on victory.
They prosper without boasting,
or domineering, or arrogance,
prosper because they can't help it,
prosper without violence.

Things flourish then perish.
Not the Way.
What's not the Way
soon ends.

This first direct statement of Lao Tzu's pacifism is connected in
thought to the previous poem and leads directly to the next.

The last verse is enigmatic: "Things flourish then perish"—How
can this supremely natural sequence not be the Way? I offer my understanding of it in the note on the page with chapter 55, where nearly the
same phrase occurs.

AGAINST WAR

31

Even the best weapon
is an unhappy tool,
hateful to living things.
So the follower of the Way
stays away from it.

Weapons are unhappy tools,
not chosen by thoughtful people,
to be used only when there is no choice,
and with a calm, still mind,
without enjoyment.
To enjoy using weapons
is to enjoy killing people,
and to enjoy killing people
is to lose your share in the common good.

It is right that the murder of many people
be mourned and lamented.
It is right that a victor in war
be received with funeral ceremonies.

SACRED POWER

The way goes on forever nameless.
Uncut wood, nothing important,
yet nobody under heaven
dare try to carve it.
If rulers and leaders could use it,
the ten thousand things
would gather in homage,
heaven and earth would drop sweet dew,
and people, without being ordered,
would be fair to one another.

To order, to govern,
is to begin naming;
when names proliferate
it's time to stop.
If you know when to stop
you're in no danger.

The Way in the world
is as a stream to a valley,
a river to the sea.

The second verse connects the uncut, the uncarved, the unusable, to the idea of the unnamed presented in the first chapter: "name's the mother of the ten thousand things." You have to make order, you have to make distinctions, but you also have to know when to stop before you've lost the whole in the multiplicity of parts. The simplicity or singleness of the Way is that of water, which always rejoins itself.

KINDS OF POWER

33

Knowing other people is intelligence,
knowing yourself is wisdom.
Overcoming others takes strength,
overcoming yourself takes greatness.
Contentment is wealth.

Boldly pushing forward takes resolution.
Staying put keeps you in position.

To live till you die
is to live long enough.

PERFECT TRUST

The Great Way runs
to left, to right,
the ten thousand things
depending on it,
living on it,
accepted by it.

34

Doing its work,
it goes unnamed.
Clothing and feeding
the ten thousand things,
it lays no claim on them
and asks nothing of them.
Call it a small matter.
The ten thousand things
return to it,
though it lays no claim on them.
Call it great.

So the wise soul
without great doings
achieves greatness.

HUMANE POWER

Hold fast to the great thought
and all the world will come to you,
harmless, peaceable, serene.

Walking around, we stop
for music, for food.
But if you taste the Way
it's flat, insipid.
It looks like nothing much,
it sounds like nothing much.
And yet you can't get enough of it.

THE SMALL DARK LIGHT

What seeks to shrink
must first have grown;
what seeks weakness
surely was strong.
What seeks its ruin
must first have risen;
what seeks to take
has surely given.

This is called the small dark light:
the soft, the weak prevail
over the hard, the strong.

There is a third stanza in all the texts:

Fish should stay underwater:
the real means of rule
should be kept dark.

Or, more literally, "the State's sharp weapons ought not to be shown to
the people." This Machiavellian truism seems such an anticlimax to
the great theme stated in the first verses that I treat it as an intrusion,
perhaps a commentator's practical example of "the small dark light."

OVER ALL

37

The Way never does anything,
and everything gets done.
If those in power could hold to the Way,
the ten thousand things
would look after themselves.
If even so they tried to act,
I'd quiet them with the nameless,
the natural.

In the unnamed, in the unshapen,
is not wanting.
In not wanting is stillness.
In stillness all under heaven rests.

Here the themes of not doing and not wanting, the unnamed and the
unshapen, recur together in one pure legato. It is wonderful how by
negatives and privatives Lao Tzu gives a sense of serene, inexhaustible
fullness of being.

Book Two

TALKING ABOUT POWER

Great power, not clinging to power,
has true power.
Lesser power, clinging to power,
lacks true power.
Great power, doing nothing,
has nothing to do.
Lesser power, doing nothing,
has an end in view.

The good the truly good do
has no end in view.
The right the very righteous do
has an end in view.
And those who act in true obedience to law
roll up their sleeves
and make the disobedient obey.

38

So: when we lose the Way we find power;
losing power we find goodness;
losing goodness we find righteousness;
losing righteousness we're left with obedience.

Obedience to law is the dry husk
of loyalty and good faith.
Opinion is the barren flower of the Way,
the beginning of ignorance.

So great-minded people
abide in the kernel not the husk,
in the fruit not the flower,
letting the one go, keeping the other.

A vast, dense argument in a minimum of words, this poem lays out the
Taoist values in steeply descending order: the Way and its power; goodness (humane feeling); righteousness (morality); and—a very distant
last—obedience (law and order). The word I render as "opinion" can be
read as "knowing too soon": the mind obeying orders, judging before
the evidence is in, closed to fruitful perception and learning.

INTEGRITY

Those who of old got to be whole:

Heaven through its wholeness is pure;
earth through its wholeness is steady;
spirit through its wholeness is potent;
the valley through its wholeness flows with rivers;
the ten thousand things through their wholeness
    live;
rulers through their wholeness have authority.
Their wholeness makes them what they are.

Without what makes it pure, heaven would
    disintegrate;
without what steadies it, earth would crack apart;
without what makes it potent, spirit would fail;
without what fills it, the valley would run dry;
without what quickens them, the ten thousand
    things would die;
without what authorizes them, rulers would fall.

The root of the noble is in the common,
the high stands on what's below.
Princes and kings call themselves
"orphans, widowers, beggars,"
to get themselves rooted in the dirt.

A multiplicity of riches
is poverty.
Jade is praised as precious,
but its strength is being stone.

BY NO MEANS

40

Return is how the Way moves.
Weakness is how the Way works.

Heaven and earth and the ten thousand things
are born of being.
Being is born of nothing.

ON AND OFF

Thoughtful people hear about the Way
and try hard to follow it.
Ordinary people hear about the Way
and wander onto it and off it.
Thoughtless people hear about the Way
and make jokes about it.
It wouldn't be the Way
if there weren't jokes about it.

So they say:
The Way's brightness looks like darkness;
advancing on the Way feels like retreating;
the plain Way seems hard going.
The height of power seems a valley;
the amplest power seems not enough;
the firmest power seems feeble.
Perfect whiteness looks dirty.
The pure and simple looks chaotic.

The great square has no corners.
The great vessel is never finished.
The great tone is barely heard.
The great thought can't be thought.

The Way is hidden
in its namelessness.
But only the Way
begins, sustains, fulfills.

CHILDREN OF THE WAY

42

The Way bears one.
The one bears two.
The two bear three.
The three bear the ten thousand things.
The ten thousand things
carry the yin on their shoulders
and hold in their arms the yang,
whose interplay of energy
makes harmony.

People despise
orphans, widowers, outcasts.
Yet that's what kings and rulers call themselves.
Whatever you lose, you've won.
Whatever you win, you've lost.

What others teach, I say too:
violence and aggression
destroy themselves.
My teaching rests on that.

Beginning with a pocket cosmology, this chapter demonstrates the "interplay of energy" of yin and yang by showing how low and high, winning and losing, destruction and self-destruction, reverse themselves, each turning into its seeming opposite.

WATER AND STONE

What's softest in the world
rushes and runs
over what's hardest in the world.

The immaterial
enters
the impenetrable.

So I know the good in not doing.

The wordless teaching,
the profit in not doing—
not many people understand it.

43

FAME AND FORTUNE

44

Which is nearer,
name or self?
Which is dearer,
self or wealth?
Which gives more pain,
loss or gain?

All you grasp will be thrown away.
All you hoard will be utterly lost.

Contentment keeps disgrace away.
Restraint keeps you out of danger
so you can go on for a long, long time.

REAL POWER

What's perfectly whole seems flawed,
but you can use it forever.
What's perfectly full seems empty,
but you can't use it up.

45

True straightness looks crooked.
Great skill looks clumsy.
Real eloquence seems to stammer.

To be comfortable in the cold, keep moving;
to be comfortable in the heat, hold still;
to be comfortable in the world, stay calm and clear.

WANTING LESS

46

When the world's on the Way,
they use horses to haul manure.
When the world gets off the Way,
they breed warhorses on the common.

The greatest evil: wanting more.
The worst luck: discontent.
Greed's the curse of life.

To know enough's enough
is enough to know.

LOOKING FAR

You don't have to go out the door
to know what goes on in the world.
You don't have to look out the window
to see the way of heaven.
The farther you go,
the less you know.

So the wise soul
doesn't go, but knows;
doesn't look, but sees;
doesn't do, but gets it done.

We tend to expect great things from "seeing the world" and "getting experience." A Roman poet remarked that travelers change their sky but not their soul. Other poets, untraveled and inexperienced, Emily Brontë and Emily Dickinson, prove Lao Tzu's point: it's the inner eye that really sees the world.

UNLEARNING

Studying and learning daily you grow larger.
Following the Way daily you shrink.
You get smaller and smaller.
So you arrive at not doing.
You do nothing and nothing's not done.

To run things,
don't fuss with them.
Nobody who fusses
is fit to run things.

The word *shi* in the second stanza, my "fuss," is troublesome to the
translators. Carus's quite legitimate translation of it is "diplomacy,"
which would give a stanza I like very much:

To run things,
be undiplomatic.
No diplomat
is fit to run things.

TRUST AND POWER

The wise have no mind of their own,
finding it in the minds
of ordinary people.

They're good to good people
and they're good to bad people.
Power is goodness.
They trust people of good faith
and they trust people of bad faith.
Power is trust.

They mingle their life with the world,
they mix their mind up with the world.
Ordinary people look after them.
Wise souls are children.

The next to last line is usually read as saying that ordinary people watch
and listen to wise people. But Lao Tzu has already told us that most of
us wander on and off the Way and don't know a sage from a sandpile.
And surely the quiet Taoist is not a media pundit.

Similarly, the last line is taken to mean that the wise treat ordinary people like children. This is patronizing, and makes hash out of
the first verse. I read it to mean that the truly wise are looked after (or
looked upon) like children because they're trusting, unprejudiced, and
don't hold themselves above or apart from ordinary life.

LOVE OF LIFE

50

To look for life
is to find death.
The thirteen organs of our living
are the thirteen organs of our dying.
Why are the organs of our life
where death enters us?
Because we hold too hard to living.

So I've heard
if you live in the right way,
when you cross country
you needn't fear to meet a mad bull or a tiger;
when you're in a battle
you needn't fear the weapons.
The bull would find nowhere to jab its horns,
the tiger nowhere to stick its claws,
the sword nowhere for its point to go.
Why? Because there's nowhere in you
for death to enter.

NATURE, NURTURE

The Way bears them;
power nurtures them;
their own being shapes them;
their own energy completes them.
And not one of the ten thousand things
fails to hold the Way sacred
or to obey its power.

Their reverence for the Way
and obedience to its power
are unforced and always natural.
For the Way gives them life;
its power nourishes them,
mothers and feeds them,
completes and matures them,
looks after them, protects them.

To have without possessing,
do without claiming,
lead without controlling:
this is mysterious power.

BACK TO THE BEGINNING

52

The beginning of everything
is the mother of everything.
Truly to know the mother
is to know her children,
and truly to know the children
is to turn back to the mother.
The body comes to its ending
but there is nothing to fear.

Close the openings,
shut the doors,
and to the end of life
nothing will trouble you.
Open the openings,
be busy with business,
and to the end of life
nothing can help you.

Insight sees the insignificant.
Strength knows how to yield.
Use the way's light, return to its insight,
and so keep from going too far.
That's how to practice what's forever.

This chapter on the themes of return and centering makes circles
within itself and throughout the book, returning to phrases from other
poems, turning them round the center. A center which is everywhere, a
circle whose circumference is infinite. . . .

INSIGHT

If my mind's modest,
I walk the great way.
Arrogance
is all I fear.

The great way is low and plain,
but people like shortcuts over the mountains.

The palace is full of splendor
and the fields are full of weeds
and the granaries are full of nothing.

People wearing ornaments and fancy clothes,
carrying weapons,
drinking a lot and eating a lot,
having a lot of things, a lot of money:
shameless thieves.
Surely their way
isn't the way.

So much for capitalism.

SOME RULES

54

Well planted is not uprooted,
well kept is not lost.
The offerings of the generations
to the ancestors will not cease.

To follow the way yourself is real power.
To follow it in the family is abundant power.
To follow it in the community is steady power.
To follow it in the whole country is lasting power.
To follow it in the world is universal power.

So in myself I see what self is,
in my household I see what family is,
in my town I see what community is,
in my nation I see what a country is,
in the world I see what is under heaven.

How do I know the world is so?
By this.

I follow Waley's interpretation of this chapter. It is Tao that plants and
keeps; the various kinds of power belong to Tao; and finally in myself I
see the Tao of self, and so on.

THE SIGN OF THE MYSTERIOUS

Being full of power
is like being a baby.
Scorpions don't sting,
tigers don't attack,
eagles don't strike.
Soft bones, weak muscles,
but a firm grasp.
Ignorant of the intercourse
of man and woman,
yet the baby penis is erect.
True and perfect energy!
All day long screaming and crying,
but never getting hoarse.
True and perfect harmony!

55

To know harmony
is to know what's eternal.
To know what's eternal
is enlightenment.
Increase of life is full of portent:
the strong heart exhausts the vital breath.
The full-grown is on the edge of age.
Not the Way.
What's not the Way soon dies.

As a model for the Taoist, the baby is in many ways ideal: totally un-altruistic, not interested in politics, business, or the proprieties, weak, soft, and able to scream placidly for hours without wearing itself out (its parents are another matter). The baby's unawareness of poisonous insects and carnivorous beasts means that such dangers simply do not exist for it. (Again, its parents are a different case.)

As a metaphor of the Tao, the baby embodies the eternal begin-ning, the ever-springing source. "We come, trailing clouds of glory," Wordsworth says; and Hopkins, "There lives the dearest freshness deep down things." No Peter Pan–ish refusal to grow up is involved, no hunt for the fountain of youth. What is eternal *is* forever young, never grows old. But we are not eternal.

It is in this sense that I understand how the natural, inevitable cycle of youth, growth, mature vigor, age, and decay can be "not the Way." The Way is more than the cycle of any individual life. We rise, flourish, fail. The Way never fails. We are waves. It is the sea.

MYSTERIES OF POWER

Who knows
doesn't talk.
Who talks
doesn't know.
Closing the openings,
shutting doors,

blunting edge,
loosing bond,
dimming light,
be one with the dust of the way.
So you come to the deep sameness.

Then you can't be controlled by love
or by rejection.
You can't be controlled by profit
or by loss.
You can't be controlled by praise
or by humiliation.
Then you have honor under heaven.

BEING SIMPLE

57

Run the country by doing what's expected.
Win the war by doing the unexpected.
Control the world by doing nothing.
How do I know that?
By this.

The more restrictions and prohibitions in the world,
the poorer people get.
The more experts the country has
the more of a mess it's in.
The more ingenious the skillful are,
the more monstrous their inventions.
The louder the call for law and order,
the more the thieves and con men multiply.

A strong political statement of the central idea of *wu wei*, not doing, inaction.

My "monstrous" is literally "new." New is strange, and strange is uncanny. New is bad. Lao Tzu is deeply and firmly against changing things, particularly in the name of progress. He would make an Iowa farmer look flighty. I don't think he is exactly anti-intellectual, but he considers most uses of the intellect to be pernicious, and all plans for

So a wise leader might say:
I practice inaction, and the people look after
    themselves.
I love to be quiet, and the people themselves find
    justice.
I don't do business, and the people prosper on their
    own.
I don't have wants, and the people themselves are
    uncut wood.

---

improving things to be disastrous. Yet he's not a pessimist. No pessimist would say that people are able to look after themselves, be just, and
prosper on their own. No anarchist can be a pessimist.

Uncut wood—here likened to the human soul—the uncut, uncarved, unshaped, unpolished, native, natural stuff is better than
anything that can be made out of it. Anything done to it deforms and
lessens it. Its potentiality is infinite. Its uses are trivial.

LIVING WITH CHANGE

58

When the government's dull and confused,
the people are placid.
When the government's sharp and keen,
the people are discontented.
Alas! misery lies under happiness,
and happiness sits on misery, alas!
Who knows where it will end?
Nothing is certain.

The normal changes into the monstrous,
the fortunate into the unfortunate,
and our bewilderment
goes on and on.

And so the wise
shape without cutting,
square without sawing,
true without forcing.
They are the light that does not shine.

In the first verse, the words "dull and confused" and "sharp and keen" are, as Waley points out, the words used in chapter 20 to describe the Taoist and the non-Taoists.

In the last verse most translators say the Taoist is square but doesn't cut, shines but doesn't dazzle. Waley says that this misses the point. The point is that Taoists gain their ends *without the use of means*. That is indeed a light that does not shine—an idea that must be pondered and brooded over. A small dark light.

STAYING ON THE WAY

In looking after your life and following the way,
gather spirit.
Gather spirit early,
and so redouble power,
and so become invulnerable.

Invulnerable, unlimited,
you can do what you like with material things.
But only if you hold to the Mother of things
will you do it for long.
Have deep roots, a strong trunk.
Live long by looking long.

59

STAYING PUT

60

Rule a big country
the way you cook a small fish.

If you keep control by following the Way,
troubled spirits won't act up.
They won't lose their immaterial strength,
but they won't harm people with it,
nor will wise souls come to harm.
And so, neither harming the other,
these powers will come together in unity.

Thomas Jefferson would have liked the first stanza.

"Troubled spirits" are *kwei*, ghosts, not bad in themselves but dangerous if they possess you. Waley reads the second stanza as a warning to believers in *Realpolitik*: a ruler "possessed" by power harms both the people and his own soul. Taking it as counsel to the individual, it might mean that wise souls neither indulge nor repress the troubled spirits that may haunt them; rather, they let those spiritual energies be part of the power they find along the way.

LYING LOW

The polity of greatness
runs downhill like a river to the sea,
joining with everything,
woman to everything.

By stillness the woman
may always dominate the man,
lying quiet underneath him.

So a great country
submitting to small ones, dominates them;
so small countries,
submitting to a great one, dominate it.

Lie low to be on top,
be on top by lying low.

61

THE GIFT OF THE WAY

62

The way is the hearth and home
of the ten thousand things.
Good souls treasure it,
lost souls find shelter in it.

Fine words are for sale,
fine deeds go cheap;
even worthless people can get them.

So, at the coronation of the Son of Heaven
when the Three Ministers take office,
you might race out in a four-horse chariot
to offer a jade screen;
but wouldn't it be better to sit still
and let the Way be your offering?

Why was the Way honored
in the old days?
Wasn't it said:
Seek, you'll find it.
Hide, it will shelter you.
So it was honored under heaven.

I think the line of thought throughout the poem has to do with true
reward as opposed to dishonorable gain, true giving as opposed to fake
goods.

CONSIDER BEGINNINGS

Do without doing.
Act without action.
Savor the flavorless.
Treat the small as large,
the few as many.

Meet injury
with the power of goodness.

Study the hard while it's easy.
Do big things while they're small.
The hardest jobs in the world start out easy,
the great affairs of the world start small.

So the wise soul,
by never dealing with great things,
gets great things done.

Now, since taking things too lightly makes them
    worthless,
and taking things too easy makes them hard,
the wise soul,
by treating the easy as hard,
doesn't find anything hard.

Waley says that this charmingly complex chapter plays with two proverbs. "Requite injuries with good deeds" is the first. The word *te*, here meaning goodness or good deeds, is the same word Lao Tzu uses for the Power of the Way. ("Power is goodness," he says in chapter 49.) So, having neatly annexed the Golden Rule, he goes on to the proverb about "taking things too lightly" and plays paradox with it.

MINDFUL OF LITTLE THINGS

64

It's easy to keep hold of what hasn't stirred,
easy to plan what hasn't occurred.
It's easy to shatter delicate things,
easy to scatter little things.
Do things before they happen.
Get them straight before they get mixed up.

The tree you can't reach your arms around
grew from a tiny seedling.
The nine-story tower rises
from a heap of clay.
The ten-thousand-mile journey
begins beneath your foot.

Do, and do wrong;
Hold on, and lose.
Not doing, the wise soul
doesn't do it wrong,
and not holding on,
doesn't lose it.
(In all their undertakings,
it's just as they're almost finished
that people go wrong.
Mind the end as the beginning,
then it won't go wrong.)

That's why the wise
want not to want,
care nothing for hard-won treasures,
learn not to be learned,
turn back to what people overlooked.
They go along with things as they are,
but don't presume to act.

ONE POWER

Once upon a time
those who ruled according to the Way
didn't use it to make people knowing
but to keep them unknowing.

People get hard to manage
when they know too much.
Whoever rules by intellect
is a curse upon the land.
Whoever rules by ignorance
is a blessing on it.
To understand these things
is to have a pattern and a model,
and to understand the pattern and the model
is mysterious power.

Mysterious power
goes deep.
It reaches far.
It follows things back,
clear back to the great oneness.

Where shall we find a ruler wise enough to know what to teach and
what to withhold? "Once upon a time," maybe, in the days of myth and
legend, as a pattern, a model, an ideal?

The knowledge and the ignorance or unknowing Lao Tzu speaks
of may or may not refer to what we think of as education. In the last
stanza, by power he evidently does not mean political power at all, but
something vastly different, a unity with the power of the Tao itself.

This is a *mystical* statement about *government*—and in our minds
those two realms are worlds apart. I cannot make the leap between
them. I can only ponder it.

LOWDOWN

Lakes and rivers are lords of the hundred valleys.
Why? Because they'll go lower.
So they're the lords of the hundred valleys.

Just so, a wise soul,
wanting to be above other people,
talks to them from below
and to guide them
follows them.

And so the wise soul
predominates without dominating,
and leads without misleading.
And people don't get tired
of enjoying and praising
one who, not competing,
has in all the world
no competitor.

One of the things I love in Lao Tzu is his good cheer, as in this poem, which while giving good counsel is itself a praise and enjoyment of the spirit of yin, the water-soul that yields, follows, eludes, and leads on, dancing in the hundred valleys.

THREE TREASURES

67

Everybody says my way is great
but improbable.

All greatness
is improbable.
What's probable
is tedious and petty.

I have three treasures.
I keep and treasure them.
The first, mercy,
the second, moderation,
the third, modesty.
If you're merciful you can be brave,
if you're moderate you can be generous,
and if you don't presume to lead
you can lead the high and mighty.

But to be brave without compassion,
or generous without self-restraint,
or to take the lead,
is fatal.

Compassion wins the battle
and holds the fort;
it is the bulwark set
around those heaven helps.

The first two verses of this chapter are a joy to me.

The three final verses are closely connected in thought to the next two chapters, which may be read as a single meditation on mercy, moderation, and modesty, on the use of strength, on victory and defeat.

HEAVEN'S LEAD

68

The best captain doesn't rush in front.
The fiercest fighter doesn't bluster.
The big winner isn't competing.
The best boss takes a low footing.
This is the power of noncompetition.
This is the right use of ability.
To follow heaven's lead
has always been the best way.

USING MYSTERY

The expert in warfare says:
Rather than dare make the attack
I'd take the attack;
rather than dare advance an inch
I'd retreat a foot.

It's called marching without marching,
rolling up your sleeves without flexing your muscles,
being armed without weapons,
giving the attacker no opponent.
Nothing's worse than attacking what yields.
To attack what yields is to throw away the prize.

So, when matched armies meet,
the one who comes to grief
is the true victor.

A piece of sound tactical advice (practiced by the martial arts, such as Aikido, and by underground resistance and guerrilla forces), which leads to a profound moral warning. The prize thrown away by the aggressor is compassion. The yielder, the griever, the mourner, keeps that prize. The game is loser take all.

BEING OBSCURE

70

My words are so easy to understand,
so easy to follow,

and yet nobody in the world
understands or follows them.

Words come from an ancestry,
deeds from a mastery:
when these are unknown, so am I.

In my obscurity
is my value.
That's why the wise
wear their jade under common clothes.

THE SICK MIND

To know without knowing is best.
Not knowing without knowing it is sick.

To be sick of sickness
is the only cure.

The wise aren't sick.
They're sick of sickness,
so they're well.

What you know without knowing you know it is the right kind of knowledge. Any other kind (conviction, theory, dogmatic belief, opinion)
isn't the right kind, and if you don't know that, you'll lose the Way. This
chapter is an example of exactly what Lao Tzu was talking about in the
last one—obscure clarity, well-concealed jade.

THE RIGHT FEAR

72

When we don't fear what we should fear
we are in fearful danger.
We ought not to live in narrow houses,
we ought not to do stupid work.

If we don't accept stupidity
we won't act stupidly.
So, wise souls know but don't show themselves,
look after but don't prize themselves,
letting the one go, keeping the other.

DARING TO DO

Brave daring leads to death.
Brave caution leads to life.
The choice can be the right one
or the wrong one.

Who will interpret
the judgment of heaven?
Even the wise soul
finds it hard.

The way of heaven
doesn't compete
yet wins handily,
doesn't speak
yet answers fully,
doesn't summon
yet attracts.
It acts
perfectly easily.

The net of heaven
is vast, vast,
wide-meshed,
yet misses nothing.

73

THE LORD OF SLAUGHTER

74

When normal, decent people don't fear death,
how can you use death to frighten them?
Even when they have a normal fear of death,
who of us dare take and kill the one who doesn't?
When people are normal and decent and
    death-fearing,
there's always an executioner.
To take the place of that executioner
is to take the place of the great carpenter.
People who cut the great carpenter's wood
seldom get off with their hands unhurt.

To Lao Tzu, not to fear dying and not to fear killing are equally unnatural and antisocial. Who are we to forestall the judgment of heaven or nature, to usurp the role of "the executioner"? "The Lord of Slaughter" is Waley's grand translation.

GREED

People are starving.
The rich gobble taxes,
that's why people are starving.

People rebel.
The rich oppress them,
that's why people rebel.

People hold life cheap.
The rich make it too costly,
that's why people hold it cheap.

But those who don't live for the sake of living
are worth more than the wealth-seekers.

How many hundreds of years ago was this book written? And yet still this chapter must be written in the present tense.

HARDNESS

Living people
are soft and tender.
Corpses are hard and stiff.
The ten thousand things,
the living grass, the trees,
are soft, pliant.
Dead, they're dry and brittle.

So hardness and stiffness
go with death;
tenderness, softness,
go with life.

And the hard sword fails,
the stiff tree's felled.
The hard and great go under.
The soft and weak stay up.

In an age when hardness is supposed to be the essence of strength, and
even the beauty of women is reduced nearly to the bone, I welcome this
reminder that tanks and tombstones are not very adequate role models,
and that to be alive is to be vulnerable.

THE BOW

The Way of heaven
is like a bow bent to shoot:
its top end brought down,
its lower end raised up.
It brings the high down,
lifts the low,
takes from those who have,
gives to those who have not.

Such is the Way of heaven,
taking from people who have,
giving to people who have not.
Not so the human way:
it takes from those who have not
to fill up those who have.
Who has enough to fill up everybody?
Only those who have the Way.

So the wise
do without claiming,
achieve without asserting,
wishing not to show their worth.

PARADOXES

78

Nothing in the world
is as soft, as weak, as water;
nothing else can wear away
the hard, the strong,
and remain unaltered.
Soft overcomes hard,
weak overcomes strong.
Everybody knows it,
nobody uses the knowledge.

So the wise say:
By bearing common defilements
you become a sacrificer at the altar of earth;
by bearing common evils
you become a lord of the world.

Right words sound wrong.

KEEPING THE CONTRACT

After a great enmity is settled
some enmity always remains.
How to make peace?
Wise souls keep their part of the contract
and don't make demands on others.
People whose power is real fulfill their obligations;
people whose power is hollow insist on their claims.

The Way of heaven plays no favorites.
It stays with the good.

This chapter is equally relevant to private relationships and to political treaties. Its realistic morality is based on a mystical perception of the fullness of the Way.

FREEDOM

80

Let there be a little country without many people.
Let them have tools that do the work of ten or a
hundred,
and never use them.
Let them be mindful of death
and disinclined to long journeys.
They'd have ships and carriages,
but no place to go.
They'd have armor and weapons,
but no parades.
Instead of writing,
they might go back to using knotted cords.
They'd enjoy eating,
take pleasure in clothes,
be happy with their houses,
devoted to their customs.

The next little country might be so close
the people could hear cocks crowing
and dogs barking there,
but they'd get old and die
without ever having been there.

Waley says this endearing and enduring vision "can be understood in
the past, present, or future tense, as the reader desires." This is always
true of the vision of the golden age, the humane society.

Christian or Cartesian dualism, the division of spirit or mind from
the material body and world, existed long before Christianity or Des-
cartes and was never limited to Western thought (though it is the "cra-
ziness" or "sickness" that many people under Western domination see
in Western civilization). Lao Tzu thinks the materialistic dualist, who
tries to ignore the body and live in the head, and the religious dualist,
who despises the body and lives for a reward in heaven, are both dangerous and in danger. So, enjoy your life, he says; live in your body, you
are your body; where else is there to go? Heaven and earth are one. As
you walk the streets of your town you walk on the Way of heaven.

TELLING IT TRUE

81

True words aren't charming,
charming words aren't true.
Good people aren't contentious,
contentious people aren't good.
People who know aren't learned,
learned people don't know.

Wise souls don't hoard;
the more they do for others the more they have,
the more they give the richer they are.
The Way of heaven profits without destroying.
Doing without outdoing
is the Way of the wise.

Notes

Concerning This Version

This is a rendition, not a translation. I do not know any Chinese. I could approach the text at all only because Paul Carus, in his 1898 translation of the *Tao Te Ching*, printed the Chinese text with each character followed by a transliteration and a translation. My gratitude to him is unending.

To have the text thus made accessible was not only to have a Rosetta Stone for the book itself, but also to have a touchstone for comparing other English translations one with another. If I could focus on which word the translators were interpreting, I could begin to understand why they made the choice they did. I could compare various interpretations and see why they varied so tremendously; could see how much explanation, sometimes how much bias, was included in the translation; could discover for myself that several English meanings might lead me back to the same Chinese word. And, finally, for all my ignorance of the language, I could gain an intuition of the style, the gait and cadence, of the original, necessary to my ear and conscience if I was to try to reproduce it in English.

Without the access to the text that the Carus edition gave me, I would have been defeated by the differences among the translations, and could never have thought of following them as guides towards a version of my own. As it was, working from Carus's text, I learned how to let them lead me into it, always using their knowledge, their scholarship, their decisions, as my light in darkness.

When you try to follow the Way, even if you wander off it all the time, good things happen though you do not deserve them. My work on the *Tao Te Ching* was very wandering indeed. I started in my twenties with a few chapters. Every decade or so I'd do another bit, and tell myself I'd sit down and really get to it, some day. The undeserved good thing that happened was that a true and genuine scholar of ancient Chinese and of Lao Tzu, Dr. J. P. Seaton of the University of North Carolina, saw some of my versions of bits of the *Tao Te Ching* (scurvily quoted without attribution by myself). He reprinted them with honor, and asked me for more. I do not think he knew what he was getting into. Of his invaluable teaching, his encouragement, his generosity, I can say only what Lao Tzu says at the end of the book:

> Wise souls don't hoard;
> the more they do for others the more they have,
> the more they give the richer they are.

Sources

Though the *Tao Te Ching* has been translated into English very much more often than any other Chinese classic, indeed almost overwhelmingly often, it wasn't easy to get hold of more than a few of these versions until quite recently.

Carus's word-for-word Chinese-to-English was endlessly valuable to me, but his actual translation wasn't very satisfactory. "Reason" as a translation of Tao did not ring true. I always looked at any translation of the book I found and had a go at it. The language of some was so obscure as to make me feel the book must be beyond Western comprehension. (James Legge's version was one of these, though I did find the title for a book of mine, *The Lathe of Heaven*, in Legge. Years later, Joseph Needham, the great scholar of Chinese science and technology, wrote to tell me in the kindest, most unreproachful fashion that Legge was a bit off on that one; when *Chuang Tzu* was written the lathe hadn't been invented.)

Listed roughly in the order of their usefulness to me, these are the translations that I collected over the years and came to trust in one way or another and to use as my exemplars and guides:

Paul Carus. *Lao-Tze's Tao-Teh-King.* Open Court Publishing Company, 1898. The book has recently been republished, but the editors chose to omit its unique and most valuable element, the character-by-character romanization and translation.

Arthur Waley. *The Way and Its Power: A Study of the Tao Tê Ching and Its Place in Chinese Thought.* First published in 1958; I have the Grove edition of 1968. Though Waley's translation is political where mine is poetical, his broad and profound knowledge of Chinese thought and his acutely sensitive tact as a translator were what I always turned to when in doubt, always finding secure guidance and illumination.

Robert G. Henricks. *Te-Tao Ching: Lao-Tzu, translated from the Ma-wang-tui texts.* Modern Library, 1993. It was exciting to find that new texts had been discovered; it was exciting to find their first English translation an outstanding work of scholarship, written in plain, elegant language, as transparent to the original as it could be.

Gia-Fu Feng and Jane English. *Tao Te Ching.* First published 1972; I have the Vintage edition of 1989. Arising from a sympathetic and informed understanding, this is literarily the most satisfying recent translation I have found, terse, clear, and simple.

D. C. Lau. *Lao Tzu Tao Te Ching.* First published 1963; I have the Penguin edition of 1971. A clear, deeply thoughtful translation, a most valuable reference.

Lau has also translated the *Ma wang tui* text for Everyman's Library (Knopf, 1994).

Michael Lafargue. *The Tao of the Tao Te Ching.* State University of New York Press, 1992.

Tam C. Gibbs and Man-jan Cheng. *Lao-Tzu: "My words are very easy to understand."* North Atlantic Books, 1981.

These books, though somewhat quirky, each proved useful in casting a different light on knotty bits and obscure places in the text and suggesting alternative readings or word choices.

Witter Bynner. *The Way of Life According to Lao Tzu.* Capricorn Books, 1944. In the dedication to his friend Kiang Kang-hu, Bynner quotes him: "It is impossible to translate it without an interpretation. Most of the translations were based on the interpretations of commentators, but you chiefly took its interpretation from your own insight . . . so the translation could be very close to the original text even without knowledge of the words." This is true of Bynner's very free, poetic "American Version," and its truth helped give me the courage to work on my own American Version fifty years later. I did not refer often to Bynner while I worked, because his style is very different from mine and his vivid language might have controlled my own rather than freeing it. But I am most grateful to him.

I started out using translations by Stephen Mitchell and Chang Chung-yuan, but found them not useful. Since I began working seriously on this version, so many *Tao Te Chings* have appeared or reappeared that one begins to wonder if Lao Tzu has more translators than he has readers. I have looked hopefully into many, but none of the new versions seems to improve in any way on Waley, Henricks, Lau, or Feng-English, and many of them blur the language into dullness and vagueness. Lao Tzu is tough-minded. He is tender-minded. He is never, under any circumstances, squashy-minded. By confusing mysticism with imprecision, such versions betray the spirit of the book and its marvelously pungent, laconic, beautiful language.*

---

*If you want to know more about Taoism, or would like some help and guidance in reading the *Tao Te Ching*, the best, soundest, clearest introduction and guide is still Holmes Welch's *Taoism: The Parting of the Way* (Boston: Beacon Press, 1957).

Notes on Some Choices of Wording

For *tao*, I mostly use "Way," sometimes "way," depending on context. "Way" in my text always represents the character *tao*.

I consistently render the character *te* as "power." "Virtue" (*virtus, vertú*) in its old sense of the inherent quality and strength of a thing or person is far closer to the mark, but that sense is pretty well lost. Applied obsessively to the virginity or monogamy of women, the word lost its own virtue. When used of persons it now almost always has a smirk or a sneer in it. This is a shame. Lao Tzu's "Power is goodness" makes precisely the identification we used to make in the word "virtue." "Power," on the other hand, is a powerful word, almost a mana-word for us. It is also a very slippery one, with many connotations. To identify it with goodness takes a special, Taoistic definition of it as a property of—the virtue of—the Way.

The phrase *t'ien hsia*, literally "under heaven," occurs many times throughout the text. More often than not I render it as "the world." It is often translatable as "the Empire"—which after all meant the world, to Lao Tzu's contemporaries. I avoid this, in order to avoid historical specificity; but often *t'ien hsia* indubitably means one's country, one's land, as in chapter 26. Elsewhere I call it the public good, the commonwealth, or the common good, and sometimes I render it literally.

The phrase *wan wuh*, occurring very frequently, means the material world, all beings, everything. I often use the traditional literal translation, "the ten thousand things," because it's lively and concrete, but at times I say "everything" or "the things of this world."

I use "wise soul" or "the wise" for the several words and phrases usually rendered as Sage, Wise Man, Saint, Great Man, and so on, and I avoid the pronoun usually associated with these terms. I wanted to make a version that doesn't limit wisdom to males, and doesn't give the impression that a follower of the Tao has to be a professional, full-time Holier-than-Thou who lives up above snowline. Unimportant, uneducated, untrained men and women can be wise souls. (I thought of using *mensch*.)

With the same intention, I often use the plural pronoun where other translations use the singular, to avoid unnecessary gendering and to keep from suggesting the idea of uniqueness, singularity. I appreciate the Chinese language for making such choices available.

Certain obscure passages and verses that change or obstruct the sense of the poems may be seen as errors or interpolations by copyists. I decided to eject some of them. My authority for doing so is nil—a poet's judgment that "this doesn't belong here." It takes nerve to drop a line that Waley has left in. My version is openly dependent on the judgment of the scholars. But my aim was to make aesthetic, intellectual, and spiritual sense, and I felt that efforts to treat material extraneous to the text as integral to it weaken its integrity. Anyhow, rejects are discussed and printed in the commentary on the page with the poem, or in the Notes.

The Titles of the Poems: Carus is one of the few translators to use titles; they are in both his Chinese text and his translation. I follow his version sometimes, and sometimes invent my own.

The Two Texts of the *Tao Te Ching*

We now have two versions of the *Tao Te Ching*: the texts that have been standard since the third century CE, and the *Ma wang tui* texts of the mid-first century CE, not discovered till 1973. They differ in many details, but in only one major respect: the order of the two books that constitute the text.

The three words *tao te ching*, put into English without syntactical connection, are "way power classic." The usual interpretation gives the meaning of this title as something on the order of "the classic [text] about the way and [its] power." The two books are titled (in some versions) *Tao*, "The Way," and *Te*, "The Power." (I personally find that the poems do not consistently reflect that division of subject-matter.) In the *Ma wang tui*, the Power comes before the Way.

I keep the standard order, in which *tao* precedes *te*, and the famous stanza about the go-able way and the nameable name is the first chapter, not the thirty-eighth. Where there are differences in wording, I follow sometimes the standard text, sometimes Robert G. Henricks's translation of the *Ma wang tui*, whichever seemed more useful.

Notes on the Chapters

CHAPTER 1

Here, for the words in the third verse that I render "what it wants," I use the *Ma wang tui* text. The words in the standard text mean boundaries, or limits, or outcomes. This version seems to follow more comprehensibly from the preceding lines.

And yet the idea of what can be delimited or made manifest is relevant. In the last verse, the two "whose identity is mystery" may be understood to be the hidden, the unnameable, the limitless vision of the freed soul—and the manifest, the nameable, the field of vision limited by our wants. But the endlessness of all that is, and the limitation of mortal bodily life, are the same, and their sameness is the key to the door.

CHAPTER 5

As I said above, in a few of the poems I leave out lines which I find weaken the coherence of the text to the point that I believe them to be a long-ago reader's marginal notes which got incorporated in later copyings. My authority for these omissions is strictly personal and aesthetic. Here I omit the last two lines. Translations of them vary greatly; my version is:

> Mere talk runs dry.
> Best keep to the center.

CHAPTER 12

There are times Lao Tzu sounds very like Henry David Thoreau, but Lao Tzu was kinder. When Thoreau says to distrust any enterprise that requires new clothes, I distrust him. He is macho, flaunting his asceticism. Lao Tzu knows that getting all entangled with the external keeps us from the eternal, but (see chapter 80) he also understands that sometimes people like to get dressed up.

CHAPTER 13

T'ien hsia, "under heaven," i.e., the Empire, or the world: here I render it as "the public good," "the commonwealth," and "the body politic."

J. P. Seaton comments: "When Lao Tzu mentions 'the Empire' or 'all under heaven,' he does so with the assumption that all his readers know that it is a commonwealth where only the ruler who rules by virtue of virtue alone is legitimate."

CHAPTERS 17, 18, AND 19

Henricks considers these three chapters to belong together.

The last two lines of 19 are usually printed as the first two lines of 20, but Henricks thinks they belong here, and I follow him.

In 18, line 6, the words *hsiao tzu* are traditionally translated as "filial piety and paternal affection," a Confucian ideal. In that chapter Lao Tzu cites these dutiful families as a symptom of social disorder. But in chapter 19, line 4, *hsiao tzu* appears as the good that will result when people cease being moralistic. Unable to reconcile these contradictory usages, and feeling that Lao Tzu was far more likely to use Confucian language satirically than straightforwardly, I fudged the translation in chapter 19, calling it "family feeling." Evidently we aren't the only society or generation to puzzle over what a family is and ought to be.

Sometimes I translate the characters *su* and *p'u* with such words as *simple, natural*. Though the phrase "the uncarved block" has become familiar to many, yet metaphor may distance ideas and weaken a direct statement. But sometimes, as here, I use the traditional metaphors, because the context so clearly implies knowing something as an artist knows her materials, keeping hold on something solid.

CHAPTER 20

The standard texts ask what's the difference between *wei* and *o*, which might be translated "yes" and "yessir." The *Ma wang tui* has *wei* and *ho:* "yes" and "no." This is parallel with the next line ("good and bad" in the standard text, "beautiful and ugly" in the *Ma wang tui*). Here's a case where the older text surely is correct, the later ones corrupt.

In the first two lines of the second verse, the *Ma wang tui* text is perfectly clear: "A person whom everyone fears ought to be feared." The standard text is strange, obscure: "What the people fear must be feared." Yet the next lines follow from it as they don't from the *Ma wang tui*; and after much pondering I followed the standard text.

CHAPTER 23

In the second verse the word *shih*, "loss," gives trouble to all the translators. Waley calls it "the reverse of the power" and "inefficacy," and Waley's interpretations are never to be ignored. All the same, I decided to take it not as the opposite of the Way and the power, but as a kind of shadow-Way. Identify yourself with loss, failure, the obscure, the unpossessible, and you'll be at home even there.

CHAPTER 24

My version of the first four lines of the second verse doesn't follow any of the scholarly translations, and is quite unjustified, but at least, unlike them, it makes sense without horrible verbal contortions.

CHAPTER 25

In all the texts, the fourth verse reads:

> So they say: "The Way is great,
> heaven is great,
> earth is great,
> and the king is great.
> Four greatnesses in the world,
> and the king is one of them."

Yet in the next verse, which is the same series in reverse order, instead of "the king" it's "the people" or "humanity." I think a Confucian copyist slipped the king in. The king garbles the sense of the poem and goes against the spirit of the book. I dethroned him.

The last words of the chapter, *tzu jan*, which I render "what is," bear many interpretations. Waley translates them as "the Self-So," glossing them as "the unconditioned" or "what is so of itself"; Henricks, "what is so on its own"; Lau, "that which is naturally so"; Gibbs-Cheng, "Nature"; Feng-English, "what is natural"; Lafargue, "things as they are." I came out closest to Lafargue in this case.

CHAPTER 26

I follow the *Ma wang tui* text for the third verse, which fits the theme much better than the non-sequitur standard text, "Amid fine sights they sit calm and aloof." The syntax of the *Ma wang tui* also clarifies the last verse, relating it to the last verse of chapter 13.

CHAPTER 27

The first two lines of the third verse say that the not-good are the *t'zu:* "the capital" (Carus), or "the charge" (Feng-English), or "the stock in trade" (Waley), or "the raw material" (Henricks) of the good. Lafargue has "the less excellent are material for the excellent," and Gibbs-Cheng, "mediocre people have the potential to be good people." The latter two interpretations seemed the most useful to me. And so I call these makings, this raw material, "a student"—somebody learning to be or know better.

The last lines of the second and third verses are translated in wildly various ways; my "hidden light" and "deep mystery" are justified if, as I believe, Lao Tzu is signaling that his apparently simple statements have complex implications and need thinking about. Of course, this is true of everything in the book.

CHAPTER 28

"The natural" and "natural wood" are the same word, *p'u,* which I talked about in the note to chapter 19. Given the amount of cutting up and carving that goes on in the last verse (which seems a kind of footnote to the first three), we really seem to be talking about wood.

Chinese lends itself to puns, and this last verse is rife with them. Waley says that *ch'i* ("useful things") can mean "vessels" or "vassals," and *chih* can mean "carving" or "governing." A great government wouldn't chop and hack at human nature, trying to make leaders out of sow's ears. But the paradox of the last two lines surely exceeds any single interpretation.

CHAPTER 29

The phrase *t'ien hsia* occurs only in the first verse, where I translate it "the world." I begin the second verse with the literal translation of it, "under heaven." I wanted the phrase in the poem as a reminder that the world of these extremes—of hot and cold, weakness and strength, gain and loss—is the sacred object, the place under heaven.

CHAPTER 31

I have omitted certain lines included by the translators who are my sources and guides. In all the texts, the second verse begins:

> A courteous person
> in peacetime honors the left,
> in wartime, the right.

And the last verse begins:

> In celebrations the left is the place of honor,
> in mourning the right is the place of honor:
> so lesser officers stand on the left,
> the generalissimo on the right,
> just as they would at a funeral.

I consider these passages to be commentaries or marginal glosses that got copied into the text. J. P. Seaton says, "What were once supports by analogy to common ceremonial practice are now relevant only to the historian." Here they confuse the clear, powerful statement that culminates in the last four lines. The confusion already existed when the *Ma wang tui* version was written, and there seems to be no way of sorting it out now except by radical surgery.

Chapter 33

This chapter sounds like Polonius, incontrovertible but banal, until the last verse, which is a doozer. Here are some other versions of the last six words, *Sss erh pu wang che shou:*

> Carus (word for word): "[Who] dies / yet / not / perishes, / the-one / is-long-lived [immortal]."
>
> Carus's free translation: "One who may die but des not perish has life everlasting."
>
> Waley: "When one dies one is not lost; there is no other longevity."
>
> Feng-English: "To die but not to perish is to be eternally present."
>
> Henricks: "To die but not be forgotten—that's [true] long life."
>
> Bynner: "Vitality cleaves to the marrow / Leaving death behind."
>
> Lafargue: "One who dies and does not perish is truly long-lived."
>
> Gibbs-Cheng: "One who dies yet still remains has longevity."
>
> Lau: "He who lives out his days has had a long life."

Under J. P. Seaton's guidance I finally came to feel that I had a handle on the line, and that Lau's rendition was the most useful. One thing is certain, Lao Tzu is not saying that immortality or even longevity is desirable. The religion called Taoism has spent much imagination on ways to prolong life interminably or gain immortality, and the mythologized Lao Tzu was supposed to have run Methuselah a close race; but the Lao Tzu who wrote this had no truck with such notions.

Chapter 36

Wei ming—this phrase in the first line of the second verse (and the chapter title)—is tricky:

> Carus (word for word): "the secret's / explanation"; Carus's free translation: "explanation [i.e., enlightenment] of the secret"
>
> Feng-English: "perception of the nature of things"
>
> Gibbs-Cheng: "wonderfully minute and obscure, yet brilliant"
>
> Lafargue: "subtle clarity"
>
> Henricks: "subtle light"
>
> Bynner: "a man with insight"
>
> Waley: "dimming one's light"

Ming is "light" or "enlightenment." Waley explains that *wei* means obscure because very small, and also obscure because dark. I use this second meaning to make an oxymoron.

Chapter 37

The words in the first verse I translate as "the nameless, the natural" and in the next verse as "the unnamed, the unshapen" are the same four words: *wu ming chih p'u*; more literally, "the naturalness of the unnamed." "The unnamed" is a key phrase in the first chapter and elsewhere, as is "not wanting," "unwanting." *P'u* is the natural, the uncut wood, or, as Waley glosses it here, "uncarved-wood quality."

Chapter 38

The series here is of familiar Confucian principles: *jen, li, i*—"good, humane, human-hearted, altruistic";

"righteous, moral, ethical"; "laws, rites, rules, law and order." But Lao Tzu reverses and subverts the Confucian priorities.

Chien shih in the fourth verse is "premature knowledge" in Carus and "foreknowledge" in Lau, Henricks, and Waley (who explains it as part of Confucian doctrine). Henricks interprets it as having "one's mind made up before one enters a new situation about what is 'right' and 'wrong' and 'proper' and 'acceptable' and so on." Prejudice, that is, or opinion. Buddhists and Taoists agree in having a very low opinion of opinion.

CHAPTER 39

Yi, "one, the one, unity, singleness, integrity," is here translated as "whole, wholeness."

Waley explains the last two verses as comments on the first three, but their relevance is pretty tenuous. The last verse is very difficult and the translations are various and ingenious. Henricks reads the *Ma wang tui* text of the first two lines of it as meaning "too many carriages is the same as no carriage," and I picked up on the idea of multiplicity as opposed to the singleness or wholeness spoken of in the first verses. The meaning of the lines about jade seems to be anybody's guess.

CHAPTER 41

I moved the line about perfect whiteness down to keep the three lines about power together, in parallel structure with the three lines about the Way. In the last line of the second verse (and in chapters 21 and 35) I translate *hsiang* as "thought." The word connotes "form, shape, image, idea." Waley explains it as the form which is formless, the Tao which can't be tao'd.

Chapter 42

In the sixth line, does the word *fu* mean "carry on one's back" or "turn one's back on"? Lafargue is the only translator I found that made the second choice. I don't follow him because I don't think the "ten thousand things" would or can make the mistake of turning their backs on the yin to embrace only yang. (But a great many of us do make that mistake, which is why Lao Tzu keeps reminding us to value yin, the soft, the dark, the weak, earth, water, the Mother, the Valley.)

Lafargue's reading, however, lets the next stanza follow more coherently—orphans, the bereaved, the outcast are what we turn our backs on; winning is yang, losing is yin. Through loss we win. . . .

The last stanza is uncharacteristic in its didactic tone and in assimilating the teaching to a tradition. Lao Tzu usually cites "what others teach" only to dissociate himself from it. I was inclined to dismiss it as a marginal note by someone who was teaching and annotating the text. But J. P. Seaton, who does teach the text, persuaded me to keep it in the body of the poem, saying, "It's a message that for all its flat moralism does connect Taoism to Confucianism and even to Buddhism with a single solid thread—averting a hundred holy wars, if nothing else."

Chapter 44

The intense, succinct, beautiful language of the first verses of a poem is sometimes followed by a verse or two in a more didactic tone, smaller in scope, and far more prosaic. I believe some of these verses are additions, comments, and examples, copied into the manuscripts so long ago that they became holy writ. They usually have their own charm and validity, but—as here, and in chapter 39 and other places—they bring a tremendous statement down to a rather commonplace ending. But then, Lao Tzu values the commonplace.

CHAPTER 47

The last line, literally "not do, yet accomplish," is a direct statement of one of the fundamental themes of the book. When I came up with a slightly mealy version of it ("doesn't do, but it's done"), J. P. Seaton reminded me that "doing without doing is doing, not not doing."

CHAPTER 48

Shi (my "fuss," Carus's "diplomacy") is translated by Lafargue as "work," by Lau as "meddling," by Waley and Feng-English as "interference," by Henricks as "concern," by Gibbs-Cheng as "act for gain."

CHAPTER 49

Following some of Carus's interpretations, the first lines of the third verse might be read, "Wise souls live in the world carefully, handling it carefully, making their mind universal." I can't make much sense of any of the other versions except Henricks's beautiful reading:

> As for the Sage's presence in the world, he is
>   one with it.
> And with the world he merges his mind.

CHAPTER 50

Those who read *shih yu san* as "thirteen," rather than as "three out of ten," make better sense of the difficult first verse. The thirteen "companions of life" (Waley, Henricks), which I translate "organs," may be physical, the limbs and passages and cavities of the body—or physio/psychological, the emotions and sensations.

My "mad bull" occurs variously as a rhinoceros and a wild buffalo. The idea seems to be a big irritable animal with horns.

My "live in the right way" is literally "take care of your life," or "hold on to your life." The context indicates care without anxiety, holding without grasping. I read the poem as saying that if you can take life as it comes, it doesn't come at you as your enemy. Lao Tzu's "nowhere for death to enter" isn't a promise of invulnerability or immortality; his concern is how to live rightly, how to "live till you die."

CHAPTER 52

The last two lines of the first verse are the same as the last two lines of chapter 16. I wonder if some of these repetitions were insertions by people studying and copying the book, who were reminded of one poem by another and noted down the relevant lines. They are indeed relevant here, but they don't fit with perfect inevitability, as they do in chapter 16. This is of course a purely aesthetic judgment, subject to destruction by scholarship at any moment.

CHAPTER 54

Gibbs and Cheng, finding both the language and the message "discordant with the teachings of Lao Tzu," won't even discuss this chapter. Waley's reading saves it, but the listing "self, family, community, country, empire/world" (a conventional series in ancient Chinese thought), and the list of rules and results is uncharacteristically mechanical. Though he uses many commonplaces, familiar phrases, rhymed sayings, and so on, Lao Tzu's thought and language are usually more unconventional and unpredictable than this.

CHAPTER 56

Another repetition: the first four lines of the second verse are the same as the second verse of chapter 4. They carry a different weight here. I vary my translation of them in the fourth line to make it connect to the next.

Hsuan t'ung, "the deep sameness": *hsuan* is "deep" or "mysterious"; *t'ung* is variously translated "identification," "oneness," "sameness," "merging," "leveling," "assimilation." It is an important theme, met with before in chapter 49.

CHAPTER 57

The phrase "How do I know? By this," has become a kind of tag by its third repetition; but as Waley points out, it still implies intuitive knowing, beyond reason—knowing the way.

The words I translate "experts" literally mean "sharp weapons," but the term implies "pundits, know-it-alls." I was tempted to say "smart bombs," which is too cute and topical, but which would certainly lead neatly to the next lines.

CHAPTER 58

Waley points out that words in the last verse, with such meanings as "square, right, angular," are typical Confucian virtues. Henricks remarks that all these words and operations refer to carpentry. The verse is about how to cut the uncut wood without cutting it.

CHAPTER 59

Se, my "gather spirit," is variously translated "frugality," "moderation," "restraint," "being sparing," or, by Waley, "laying up a store." Evidently the core idea is that of saving.

The chapter is usually presented in the manual-for-princes mode. Waley makes sense out of it by complex technical references; other versions make only gleams of sense. To persuade or coerce it into the personal mode meant a more radical interpretation than I usually dare attempt, but Waley's reading, which points to the symbology of the breath (*ch'i*) and the "long look" of the meditator, gave me the courage to try. Here is a version closer to the conventional ones:

> In controlling people and serving heaven
> it's best to go easy.
> Going easy from the start
> is to gather power from the start,
> and gathered power keeps you safe.
>
> Safe, you can do what you like.
> Do what you like, the country's yours.
> If you can make the country's Mother yours,
> you'll last a long time.
> You'll have deep roots and a strong trunk.
> The way to live long is to look long.

CHAPTER 61

The first seven lines continue the themes of "sameness" or assimilation, and of "being woman," "being water," the uses of yin. From there on, the language goes flat, and may be interpolated commentary. There's an even feebler fourth verse:

> A big country needs more people,
> A small one needs more room.
> Each can get what it needs,
> but the big one needs to lie low.

Because the *Ma wang tui* texts are older, one longs to see them as more authentic, less corrupt. But though they are invaluable in offering variant readings, some of the variants may themselves be corruptions. In this chapter, the *Ma wang tui* reads "Small countries, submitting to a great one, are dominated," and in the next verse, "Some by lying low stay on top, but some by lying low stay on the bottom." Both versions are truisms, but the *Ma wang tui* version isn't even a Taoistic truism.

CHAPTER 62

The first and last verses hang together; the two middle verses are difficult and rather incoherent. Waley says the enigmatic second verse refers to sophists and sages who went about selling their "fine words" to the highest bidder, like our pop gurus and TV pundits.

CHAPTER 64

I think the advice about being careful at the end of an undertaking was added, perhaps to balance the advice that the right time to act is before the beginning. It confuses the argument a bit, and I put it in parentheses.

The line I give as "turn back to what people overlooked" is rendered by Lafargue as "turns back to the place all others have gone on from"; Feng-English, "brings men back to what they have lost"; Henricks, "returns to what the masses have passed by"; Waley, "turning all men back to the things they have left behind." Each version brings out a different color in the line, like different lights on an opal.

CHAPTER 65

A dictator and his censors might all too easily cite from this chapter. A democrat might agree that the more people know, the harder they are for a ruler to govern — since the more they know, the better they are at governing themselves. Anyone might agree that an intellectual agenda pursued without reality-checking is indeed a curse upon the land. From the divine right of kings through the deadly teachings of Hitler and Mao to the mumbojumbo of economists, government by theory has done endless ill. But why is Lao Tzu's alternative to it a people kept in ignorance? What kind of ignorance? Ignorance of what? Lao Tzu may be signaling us to ask such questions when he speaks of "understanding these things."

Chapter 69

Waley is my guide to the interpretation of the second verse, but I make very free with the last two lines of it. If they aren't a rather vapid statement that one should never underestimate one's foe, they must follow from what went before and lead to the extraordinary last verse. It all comes down to the last line and the word *shwai*. Carus translates it as "the weaker [the more compassionate]," and Bynner uses the word "compassion." Waley translates it as "he who does not delight in war," Henricks as "the one who feels grief," Gibbs-Cheng as "the one stung by grief," Feng-English as "the underdog," Lafargue as "the one in mourning." A man of sorrows, and acquainted with grief.

Chapter 71

I follow Henricks in choosing the *Ma wang tui* text, which has a double negative in the second line. Most other texts have "not knowing knowing is sickness."

CHAPTER 72

I take the liberty of reading this chapter as a description of what we, we ordinary people, should fear. The usual reading is in the manual-for-princes mode. In that case "what should be feared" is the ruler, the rightful authority, and the advice that follows is evidently directed to that ruler. It's certainly what William Blake would have told the oligarchs of the Industrial Revolution, who still control our lives:

> When people don't fear what should be feared
> they are in fearful danger.
> Don't make them live in narrow houses,
> don't force them to do stupid work.
>
> When they're not made stupid
> they won't act stupidly.

CHAPTER 74

I follow the *Ma wang tui* text, but make very free with the word Henricks renders as "constant [in their behavior]." If I understand Henricks' version, it says that if people were consistent in behaving normally and in fearing death, and if death were the penalty for abnormal behavior, nobody would dare behave abnormally; and so there would be no executions and no executioners. But this is not the case; as Lao Tzu says, there are times when even normal people lose their normal fear of death. So what is the poem about? I read it as saying that since we are inconsistent both in our behavior and in our fear of death, no person can rightfully take on the role of executioner, and should leave the death penalty to the judgment of heaven or nature.

Chapter 80

To dismiss this Utopia as simply regressivist or anti-technological is to miss an interesting point. These people have labor-saving machinery, ships and land vehicles, weapons of offense and defense. They "have them and don't use them." I interpret: they aren't used by them. We're used, our lives shaped and controlled, by our machines, cars, planes, weaponry, bulldozers, computers. These Taoists don't surrender their power to their creations.

The eleventh line, however, is certainly regressive if it says knotted cords are to replace written literature, history, mathematics, and so on. It might be read as saying it's best not to externalize all our thinking and remembering (as we do in writing and reading), but to keep it embodied, to think and remember with our bodies as well as our verbalizing brains.

Chapter 81

This last poem is self-reflexive, wrapping it all up tight in the first verse, then opening out again to praise the un-destructive, uncompetitive generosity of the spirit that walks on the Way.

To my mind, the best reason for following the *Ma wang tui* text in reversing the order of the books is that the whole thing ends with a chapter (37) that provides a nobler conclusion than this one. But if you reverse the order, chapter 1 turns up in the middle of the book, and I simply cannot believe that that's right. That poem is a beginning. It is the beginning.